# HBR Emotional Intelligence Series

## *How to be human at work*

The HBR Emotional Intelligence Series features smart, essential reading on the human side of professional life from the pages of *Harvard Business Review*.

<table>
<tr><td>*Authentic Leadership*</td><td>*Influence and Persuasion*</td></tr>
<tr><td>*Confidence*</td><td>*Leadership Presence*</td></tr>
<tr><td>*Dealing with Difficult People*</td><td>*Managing Your Anxiety*</td></tr>
<tr><td>*Empathy*</td><td>*Mindful Listening*</td></tr>
<tr><td>*Energy and Motivation*</td><td>*Mindfulness*</td></tr>
<tr><td>*Focus*</td><td>*Power and Impact*</td></tr>
<tr><td>*Good Habits*</td><td>*Purpose, Meaning, and Passion*</td></tr>
<tr><td>*Grit*</td><td>*Resilience*</td></tr>
<tr><td>*Happiness*</td><td>*Self-Awareness*</td></tr>
<tr><td>*Inclusion*</td><td>*Virtual EI*</td></tr>
</table>

T0054600

# Managing Your Anxiety

HBR EMOTIONAL INTELLIGENCE SERIES

# Managing
# Your Anxiety

HBR EMOTIONAL INTELLIGENCE SERIES

Harvard Business Review Press

Boston, Massachusetts

Printed in the UK by TJ Books Limited, Padstow

10  9  8  7  6  5  4  3

The web addresses referenced in this book were live and correct at the time of the book's publication but may be subject to change.

Library of Congress Cataloging-in-Publication Data

Names: Harvard Business Review Press, issuing body.
Title: Managing your anxiety.
Other titles: HBR emotional intelligence series.
Description: Boston, Massachusetts : Harvard Business Review Press,
    [2024] | Series: HBR emotional intelligence series | Includes index. |
Identifiers: LCCN 2023029100 (print) | LCCN 2023029101 (ebook) |
    ISBN 9781647825645 (paperback) | ISBN 9781647825652 (epub)
Subjects: LCSH: Anxiety. | Job stress. | Self-care, Health.
Classification: LCC BF575.A6 M233 2024 (print) |
    LCC BF575.A6 (ebook) | DDC 152.4/6—dc23/eng/20230927
LC record available at https://lccn.loc.gov/2023029100
LC ebook record available at https://lccn.loc.gov/2023029101

ISBN: 978-1-64782-564-5
eISBN: 978-1-64782-565-2

The paper used in this publication meets the requirements of the American National Standard for Permanence of Paper for Publications and Documents in Libraries and Archives Z39.48-1992.

# Contents

# Contents

# Contents

# Managing
# Your Anxiety

HBR EMOTIONAL INTELLIGENCE SERIES

# 1

# Am I Anxious or Just Stressed?

By Charlotte Lieberman

You're working on a deadline when your boss pings you. It's 3 p.m. and he wants to know if you have time to help with a project that's due by 5. You don't—you still haven't eaten lunch. "It's kind of urgent," he explains, apologizing for the late notice. A pit settles in your stomach, and your thoughts begin to race. "Of course," you reply. "I'd be happy to help." It's not like saying "no" would be any less stressful.

In your head, a voice quickly pipes in to remind you of how poorly you work under pressure. *Remember last time, that panic attack? You can't prepare an entire deck in two days, let alone two hours! Imagine how easy this would be for your coworkers. Why can't you be more like them? Face it: You're probably going to be stuck at this job forever.*

And just like that, it's 3:52 p.m., and all you've done is a lot of self-loathing. *If you weren't so busy worrying,* the voice reverberates, *you would've just started already.*

Sound familiar? Me too. I've been living with anxiety my entire life.

You might be saying to yourself, "Anxiety? I thought I was just stressed."

Stress and anxiety are related, but not synonymous states. Both are normal, adaptive responses to life's challenges—work, relationships, mortality, to name just a few—and share many symptoms, including worry, stomachaches, restlessness, muscle tension, racing thoughts, headaches, sleepless nights, or all of the above.[1]

For these reasons and more, we often use the words "anxiety" and "stress" interchangeably. Yet despite their similarities, there are important differences between the two. Determining what's going on for you is the first step toward finding relief.

# What is stress?

Stress is typically defined as a response to an external trigger, and can either be acute (a tight deadline) or chronic (persistent financial trouble). In an ideal world, the duration of the stress response corresponds with its trigger: Once a stressor has been dealt with, the body can return to its natural baseline state.

## Acute stress

Remember the pit in your stomach from before? That's an example of the stress response, which you might know better as "fight-or-flight." When you're triggered by something stressful, your brain floods your body with hormones that push you to react: Blood moves away from digestive organs and into your limbs, allowing you to move more efficiently and quickly.[2] Your heart beats faster and breathing speeds up, bringing more oxygen into the bloodstream.

Stress evolved as a survival mechanism, designed to make it easier for us to fight or flee from life-threatening triggers. Today, even though unreasonable emails do not warrant the same urgency as a hungry tiger on the savannah, our bodies don't know the difference. While stress might not feel great in the moment, it can still be helpful by motivating us to stay alert and take action when we need to.

In fact, the Yerkes-Dodson law in psychology proposes that moderate levels of stress (or what psychologists call "arousal") are optimal for peak performance. We tend to talk about this state as being "in the zone" or in "flow." Too little stress leads to low-level performance, whereas too much is a recipe for needless fight-or-flight.

## Chronic stress

Stress takes a negative turn when it doesn't fade. For many of us, the near constant stressors of modern life, which have felt both particularly intense and widespread in recent years, have led our bodies to respond as though we're under constant threat, an emotional state commonly referred to as "chronic stress."

Chronic stress can lead to various other physical and mental health issues, including high blood pressure, digestive problems, anxiety, depression, and insomnia. This is why stress management is so important.

The first step to getting your body back to baseline is pausing, taking a step away from the situation, and recognizing that your body and mind are in a state of distress. From this place of awareness, you can begin to respond more skillfully to the situation and be more compassionate with yourself.

## So, what's anxiety?

While the physiological fight-or-flight response is the defining characteristic of stress, anxiety has multiple components, including excessive thinking. The primary distinguisher is that anxiety, unlike stress, is often triggered *internally* by excessive thoughts—judgments about the past, worries about the future, and so on.

Although it's unusual to feel unprompted, out-of-the-blue anxiety, it can show up in response to a stressful situation. Take the example of the last-minute request from your boss. For some, this may trigger a "good" adaptive stress response, which motivates them to get the job done. But for others, that initial pang of stress might unleash a loop of dread, worry, and self-criticism—that fragrant potpourri of feelings is what we call anxiety.

While many think anxiety is just another way we fight with ourselves and chalk it up to a rabbit hole of worry, overthinking, and shame, it's slightly more complicated. Like stress, anxiety can be useful in the right scenarios. It is the byproduct of what psychologist Stephen Porges calls "our biological imperative toward safety." The discomfort it makes us feel was designed to alert us to something, precisely so that we listen up and protect ourselves.

Luana Marques, an associate professor of psychiatry at Harvard Medical School and president of the Anxiety and Depression Association of America, told me, "Although anxiety is uncomfortable, it may signal that something's not working. [Imagine] if you didn't have pain receptors and you touched a hot surface— you would burn. Anxiety has that same protective factor that tells you 'I need to do something differently.'"

If we listen to our anxiety—rather than try to shut it up—we give ourselves an opening to break the vicious cycle. Ask: "What's going on here? Is there a reason I'm feeling this way, and what can I do about it?"

Needless to say, this is easier said than done. In the throes of anxiety (and even stress), the frontal lobe of our brains, which is usually responsible for cognitive control, goes offline—meaning that we're less able to think critically and do things like plan, organize, think about the future, and control our own impulses. Instead, the more primal part of our brains (the amygdala) takes over. Experts call this an "amygdala hijack."

## Differentiating stress, anxiety, and an anxiety disorder

When left unchecked, both stress and anxiety can escalate into more severe mental health conditions.

Anxiety disorder, which includes generalized anxiety disorder (GAD), panic disorder, post-traumatic stress disorder (PTSD), and obsessive-compulsive disorder (OCD) is the most common mental health condition in the U.S., affecting more than 40 million Americans.[3] Globally, anxiety disorders are also the most common mental health condition, affecting up to one in 13 people.

The basic criteria for determining whether stress or anxiety have become problematic is whether they have begun adversely affecting key domains of your life—such as work or social situations. "Maybe you're having trouble sleeping, trouble concentrating, or have increased symptoms like irritability or sadness," said Marques. "As a rule of thumb, those things have to happen for enough time consistently to qualify as an anxiety disorder."

Whether or not your stress or anxiety feel manageable at a given moment is a highly personal question—especially since some degree of both is actually necessary for us to feel motivated. "Most people can actually pulse check when stress or anxiety become too much," Marques said. "When you start to see that regular interference [in your life], that's usually when it's time to seek some help."

While understanding where stress and anxiety come from, and the difference between them, won't make your feelings go away, it's the first and most important step to freeing yourself from discomfort—whether on your own or with a therapist. Because like so many things we do, feel, and think, stress and anxiety can easily become habits, well-worn paths most of us plod down on autopilot.

Make the choice to become aware of these things when they show up in yourself: how they feel, where in your body they live, what triggers them, and so on. When you do that, you're opening yourself up to curiosity. Being curious is as close as you can get to the energetic opposite of anxiety. It is expansive, generous, and humble. When you're curious, there's a whole world out there—an infinite number of paths you can take instead, including asking for support when you need it.

**CHARLOTTE LIEBERMAN** is a multidisciplinary writer, user experience leader, and certified coach. She has written about mental health in the *New York Times, Harvard Business Review, Marie Claire*, and elsewhere.

## Notes

1. "What's the Difference Between Stress and Anxiety?" American Psychological Association, last updated February 14, 2022, https://www.apa.org/topics/stress/anxiety -difference.
2. "Limbic System," GoodTherapy.org, last updated August 11, 2015, https://www.goodtherapy.org/blog/limbic -system/; "Understanding the Stress Response," Harvard Health Publishing, July 6, 2020, https://www.health .harvard.edu/staying-healthy/understanding-the-stress -response.
3. "Anxiety Disorders–Facts and Statistics," Anxiety & Depression Association of America, accessed June 8, 2023, https://adaa.org/about-adaa/press-room/facts-statistics.

Adapted from content posted on hbr.org, January 15, 2021.

# 2

# How to Manage Your Anxiety

By Charlotte Lieberman

When I was nine, I was diagnosed with anxiety disorder by my first-ever therapist. My parents dragged me into treatment after repeatedly catching me cleaning their bathroom. I didn't mind, but I was confused. I didn't see anything wrong with what I was doing: organizing their medicine cabinet by color and size, throwing out expired antibiotics and sticky bottles of cough syrup. My favorite part was wiping down the sink with warm water, feeling my worries wash away with stubble and soap scum. Cleaning gave me the sense that I could find inner order among the outer chaos— our cramped New York apartment, murmurs of my parents' struggling marriage, the growing pains of adolescence.

Now, two decades later, I still rely on cleaning as a coping mechanism for my anxiety. My current therapist encourages me to "sit with the feeling" instead, and sometimes I can tolerate it. There are mornings when I can wake up, take a shower, and go about my day with relative ease. There are also mornings, like today, when I feel imprisoned in a labyrinth of negative thoughts. Taking walks helps. Placing a heating pad on my stomach does too. For now, I am sitting with my anxiety, drinking my morning coffee, reminding myself to be grateful for my support system and the tools that help me manage.

It's all a practice.

Based on my personal experience and research, I've learned there's no one-size-fits-all when it comes to determining when anxiety becomes maladaptive and when to get help. The fact is that anxiety exists at different levels and in different ways in each of us, depending on our brain chemistry, genetic makeup, backgrounds, environments, social relationships, and so on.

Across the board, anxiety becomes problematic when it feels unmanageable—which also means different things for different people. Perhaps its intensity gets in the way of your day-to-day functioning. Maybe the feeling is so diffuse and unspecific that you feel at a loss for how to address it, and wondering only sucks you deeper into a quicksand of anxious thoughts. You might find yourself fixating on something that you know isn't a cause for worry, but you still can't help it. These are just some of the signs that you might benefit from professional mental health support. I know I have.

Whether on your own or alongside a therapist (I recommend both), the key to managing anxiety is learning to identify it, understand it, and respond to it with self-compassion. Here are a few research-based practices that can, hopefully, help you cope more skillfully with anxiety, no matter what it looks like for you.

## Identify and get to know your anxiety

From the wellness industry to tech and beyond, capitalism has influenced how we think about even our most mortal problems. Hunger, thirst, fatigue, boredom: There's an app for all of it. But framing anxiety as a "problem" that needs a quick fix can kickstart a vicious cycle you may know as "fight-or-flight." When we view our own painful emotions as a "threat" to fight or flee from, we turn ourselves into the enemy. So, rather than working against ourselves and trying to resist or run away from negative feelings, what if we simply said hello to them?

Research shows that mindfulness techniques like breath work can reduce anxiety and improve cognition.[1] They help us tap into the region of our brains responsible for awareness, concentration, and decision-making (the prefrontal cortex) and put us in a calmer, more focused state. We are able to think more clearly and make better, more thoughtful decisions, rather than relying on the part of our brains that view anxiety as a threat (the amygdala).

The next time you're spiraling—whether about work or your partner or nothing at all—pause and imagine anxiety knocking at your front door. Tell it, "One minute!" Then give yourself a moment to pause and try this breathing cycle: Inhale for four seconds, hold for four seconds, exhale for four seconds, hold for four seconds. This technique is known as box breathing, and it is a fast, effective way to calm the nervous system by tricking the mind into believing that the body is relaxed.

Once you've calmed down, imagine opening your front door and saying, "Ah, anxiety. Thanks for coming, but I'm not free right now."

The goal is to gently create distance between yourself, your thoughts, and your emotions. Pinpointing where in your body the uncomfortable feelings reside can also help. Is it a tightness in your chest or a churning in your stomach? Simply notice. By taking a step back from your discomfort, you may be able to relate to it with a bit more clarity. You gain the relief of perspective: This is an uncomfortable experience. This is not *me*.

## Choose an anchor

Routines help reduce general feelings of anxiety and are often effective antidotes for those with more serious mental health disorders.[2] Doing the same thing at regular intervals signals to our brains that we are safe. Call it a routine, a ritual, an anchor—whatever resonates.

What you choose to do is up to you. It can even be laughably simple. *I know that every day I take a walk at 12 p.m. before I eat lunch. I drink a glass of water upon waking up. I read the newspaper before I check my email.*

For me, writing three pages in my journal every morning is a nonnegotiable. This means I do it whether I feel like it or not, and knowing that I can follow through on this task—no matter what—gives me a reliable well of self-trust that I can dip into whenever anxiety tugs. Plus, writing down my thoughts is a cathartic, grounding exercise in and of itself. And it's not just true for me: Journaling is often used as a therapeutic tool for anxiety and other mental health conditions.[3]

Whatever routine you choose, make it a formal commitment. If it helps to keep you accountable, tell your partner, friend, or colleague about your routine, and ask them to check in with you weekly. Maybe write it on a sticky note and put it on your laptop. But don't make it a chore.

You may find you feel a greater sense of safety and comfort once you apply this practice. And when you fall off the wagon, try to forgive yourself and move on.

# Reframe self-discipline as a form of kindness

We are often conditioned to believe that feeling like our "best selves" results from maintaining a laundry list of #selfcare #goals. But for those of us with anxiety, self-care can actually be a major source of stress. My anxiety lends itself to perfectionism, which means I instinctively shudder at the thought of adding anything to my plate.

I long resisted the benefits of exercise, avoided having a social life, and dismissed my hobbies simply because I felt overwhelmed by the idea not just of having more "to do," but also having to do it perfectly. After work, I'd come home, eat takeout, and scroll on Instagram until my eyes fluttered shut. This, I rationalized, was self-care. Except that it made me feel terrible.

With time and the help of my therapist, I eventually learned to adopt a different attitude. Yes, self-care requires a degree of discipline. But discipline can be kind.

Yoga and meditation are two ways to practice what I call "supportive discipline." Focusing on the breath—and gently releasing distractions as they arise—requires both kindness and discipline. In Buddhism, this key tenet is roughly translated as "right effort." As a meditation teacher once explained to me, you can think of your breath like a fragile object. If you grip it too tightly, it will break. But if you completely slacken your hand, it will fall. This practice of finding and maintaining that careful balance, to me, is a great image of supportive discipline.

Of course, meditation doesn't feel great for everyone—and that's okay. There are an infinite number of ways to practice being kinder to yourself and tuning into the present moment. You could try new hobbies like brewing beer, crocheting, rollerblading, or bee-keeping. Exercising, drawing, and listening to music are evidence-based ways to reduce anxiety and regulate emotions.[4] Find what works for you. Then do it. Period.

## Visualize positive change

In the midst of anxiety, motivation to do *anything* can be the trickiest part. Try to connect to the positive feeling that will result from taking the action that feels "hard," whether that's going for a run or getting out of bed in the morning. Simply imagining success is correlated with motivation and the achievement of goals.[5]

When you're imagining how good it will feel, whatever "it" is, encourage yourself as you would a good friend. There is a robust body of recent research on the mental health benefits of "self-distancing," which researchers compare to "the experience of seeking out a friend's counsel on a difficult problem."[6] Rather than become immersed in the painful, often paralyzing feeling of anxiety, we can momentarily envision ourselves offering guidance to a good friend. *Stretch. Make fruit salad. Watch a romantic comedy.* (See the sidebar "What to Say to an Anxious Colleague.")

Anxiety is stubborn, so you'll likely try to wriggle out of the good advice your "distanced" self is giving. But try to engage in the mental role play as best as you can. "Whereas it is often challenging for the person experiencing a personal dilemma to reason objectively about their own circumstances," researchers explain, "friends are often uniquely capable of providing sage advice because they're not involved in the experience."

Imagine that! What would it feel like *not* to be involved in the experience of anxiety? Be creative.

Simple as these tips are, they may not always feel easy. They certainly don't for me. If anxiety is good

## WHAT TO SAY TO AN ANXIOUS COLLEAGUE

*By Ellen Hendriksen*

Noticed someone feeling anxious at work? Maybe they're pacing up and down the hallway or just looking restless. What if a colleague comes over to you and tells you they're anxious about a report they're submitting. How do you respond?

Don't try to offer quick fixes: "Have you tried yoga?" or "I hear lavender essential oil can work wonders." Advice like that, while well-intentioned, comes across as invalidating. Worse, offering advice creates an expert/amateur dynamic, rather than a relationship of equals. Likewise, dismissals like "Calm down," "There's nothing to be afraid of," or "Just don't worry about it" feel invalidating and unsupportive.

Instead, validate their experience: "It totally makes sense that we're all stressed right now" or "Trust me, nobody is doing their best work these days." Or consider making a workplace-appropriate disclosure

██████████████████████████████

of your own: "It's been a real challenge to juggle everything" or "The worst part for me is not knowing how or when all this will end."

Some worries are expressed as "what ifs"—"What if I don't get a raise?" or "What if my elderly parents get sick?" Know that the "what if" is rhetorical, but go ahead and inquire about an answer: "That's a scary thought. What *would* you do?" Anxiety is driven by uncertainty, and generating a plan creates certainty, which in turn can reduce anxiety. Supporting your colleague as they think through a plan of action (without proffering advice) can be helpful without invalidating their fears.

**Ellen Hendriksen** is a clinical psychologist and the author of *How to Be Yourself: Quiet Your Inner Critic and Rise Above Social Anxiety*.

Adapted from "When Anxiety Becomes Unbearable" on hbr.org, May 11, 2020 (product #H05LMS).

for anything, it is succeeding at making simple things feel complicated and insurmountable.

The bottom line? We can choose to be kinder, patient, and more compassionate with ourselves. Uncomfortable feelings will persist and subside—then persist again. The most productive thing any of us can do is show up to ourselves and others with open minds and hearts. It may not be the first priority on your to-do list, but let it be enough.

**CHARLOTTE LIEBERMAN** is a multidisciplinary writer, user experience leader, and certified coach. She has written about mental health in the *New York Times*, *Harvard Business Review*, *Marie Claire*, and elsewhere.

## Notes

1. Michael Christopher Melnychuk et al., "Coupling of Respiration and Attention via the Locus Coeruleus: Effects of Meditation and Pranayama," *Psychophysiology* 55, no. 9 (2018).
2. "Consistent Routines May Ease Bipolar Disorder," *Monitor on Psychology* 39, no. 2 (2008): 10, https://www.apa.org/monitor/feb08/consistent.

3. James W. Pennebaker, "Expressive Writing in Psychological Science," *Perspectives on Psychological Science* 13, no. 2 (2017): 226–229.

4. Elizabeth Aylett, Nicola Small, and Peter Bower, "Exercise in the Treatment of Clinical Anxiety in General Practice—A Systematic Review and Meta-Analysis," *BMC Health Services Research* 18, no. 559 (2018); Annemarie Abbing et al., "The Effectiveness of Art Therapy for Anxiety in Adults: A Systematic Review of Randomised and Non-Randomised Controlled Trials," *PLOS One* 13, no. 12 (2018), https://doi.org/10.1371/journal.pone.0208716; Martina de Witte et al., "Effects of Music Interventions on Stress-Related Outcomes: A Systematic Review and Two Meta-Analyses," *Health Psychology Review* 14, no. 2 (2020): 294–324.

5. Tim Blankert and Melvyn R. W. Hamstra, "Imagining Success: Multiple Achievement Goals and the Effectiveness of Imagery," *Basic and Applied Social Psychology* 39, no. 1 (2017): 60–67.

6. E. Kross and O. Ayduk, "Chapter Two—Self-Distancing: Theory, Research, and Current Directions," *Advances in Experimental Social Psychology* 55 (2017): 81–136.

Adapted from content posted on hbr.org, September 18, 2020.

# 3

# What Anxiety Does to Us at Work

By Alice Boyes

have an anxiety-prone brain. When presented with a new idea, my first instinct is usually to think of what could go wrong and the worst-case scenario. Whenever communication is ambiguous, the first conclusion I jump to is a negative one.

If you share these tendencies, you won't necessarily be able to change them, and nor do you need to; they're probably your hardwired defaults, and they can yield positive outcomes, such as diligence and sensitivity to others. However, you can learn to recognize when you're seeing through anxiety-tinted glasses and adjust your thinking so it doesn't limit you. Here are some common ways anxiety can cause problems at work and suggestions for how to minimize them.

## You misjudge the view others have of you

Anxious folks tend to worry that others dislike them or don't see them as talented. For instance, let's say a coworker doesn't greet you as warmly as they do others and always seems rushed in your interactions. You assume the person doesn't like you. But realistically, there are other possibilities: Perhaps they're warmer with people they know better, or their only way of socializing is to joke around and you give off a serious vibe. Because you don't feel liked, you avoid that colleague, but then they might feel snubbed and jump to the conclusion you don't like *them*!

Instead, it's important to recognize when you're interpreting an interpersonal situation without solid evidence. Equally, if not more important, is to understand that even if your colleague isn't into you (professionally speaking) you can still have a fruitful relationship.

## You're defensive about feedback

Anxious people are often driven to succeed, so they want feedback that helps them improve. But they also tend to catastrophize it and see it as an indicator they're doomed to fail. If this sounds like you, get clear about what makes it easier for you to be open to criticism. For me, this includes receiving feedback from someone whose advice I trust and who believes in my general competency/talent, hearing it sandwiched between positive comments, having it via email (so I can digest it slowly), and getting it when I ask for or expect it (to feel more in control).

The flipside of knowing how you like to get feedback is recognizing how you *don't* and figuring out a way to get more comfortable in those scenarios. For instance, I find it hard to take critiques from new people but I also find fresh perspectives very valuable, so I'm willing to tolerate the anxiety of it. It's also useful to have some canned responses for when feedback has caused your anxiety to spike, and you need time to modulate your reaction—for instance: "Those are good points. Let me go away and think them through and come up with a game plan for how to implement your suggestions."

## You avoid situations, then get perceived as difficult

We tend to avoid the things we're anxious about and then feel ashamed about the avoidance, which causes us to be unclear in our communication. This problem can manifest itself in big and small ways. Maybe you feel awkward about responding to an email so you procrastinate on it, which leaves the impression that you're unreliable, disorganized, or confusing. Or maybe your clinical-level fear of flying is making you turn down work trips.

In many cases it's best to be honest about what's causing your hesitation. You won't always receive the understanding you hope for, but transparency reduces everyone's stress, enhances trust, and is often perceived as brave and authentic.

## You react negatively to unexpected ideas

If your first thought when presented with new ideas is to consider the risks, downsides, and reasons they won't work, other people are probably picking up on your instinct and, worse, may perceive it as unwelcome negativity. Even if it's only your initial reaction, it can be demoralizing and annoying for others who do see a way to move forward.

If you're one of these naysayers, I recommend training yourself to give sandwich feedback. Make sure that your first response to a new idea is to note what's good about it. Doing this will help your brain improve at balanced thinking and benefit you overall.

You can then mention your worries, but end on a positive note. Another strategy is to delay reacting, even by only a few hours, so that when you do respond, you're giving a considered response.

Anxiety can motivate people in very positive ways: For example, fear of rejection can make you work harder at and deeply value relationships, and being sensitive, cautious, and careful can enhance your performance on difficult tasks. The better you understand how your anxiety works, the more you can maximize these positive aspects and minimize the negative so you're more accepting of yourself and better able to handle challenges that arise at work.

ALICE BOYES is a former clinical psychologist turned writer and the author of *The Healthy Mind Toolkit*, *The Anxiety Toolkit*, and *Stress-Free Productivity*.

Adapted from content posted on hbr.org, May 17, 2019
(product #H04YHD).

# 4

# Stop Asking, "What's the Worst That Could Happen?"

By Amantha Imber

Think back to a time when you tried to do something that scared you. Perhaps you had to give a high-stakes presentation in front of a big group of people. Maybe you worked up the courage to ask your boss for a raise. Or maybe you took a big risk—like quitting a toxic job without another opportunity lined up yet. Fear is a universal emotion, and it arises when we think we may experience physical or psychological harm.

If you spoke to someone about how you were feeling in the lead-up to the event that was making you fearful, chances are a well-meaning friend said to you, "Ask yourself: What's the worst that could happen?"

When I interviewed Michelle Poler (the founder of Hello Fears, a social movement that has reached over 70 million people worldwide) for my *How I Work* podcast, she told me that she, too, has heard this advice hundreds of times. Poler was doing her master's degree in branding back in 2015 when she started a project to conquer 100 fears in 100 days. She had recently moved to New York City and found that her fears were getting in the way of her truly enjoying and embracing her new home. Later, the project turned into a global movement and received coverage on NBC's *Today* show, Fox News, CBS, and CNN, to name a few.

Poler told me that, along the way, while she was conquering fears like performing stand-up comedy, cliff diving, and swimming with sharks, people often asked her, "What's the worst thing that could happen?" While Poler could concede that perhaps she wouldn't die, there were many other bad things this question brought to mind. *Maybe I won't die, but I will embarrass myself,* she would think. *I might fail. I might get rejected. I might hurt my ego and my self-esteem. There are so many things that can go wrong if I take a risk.*

The main problem with this oft-asked question is that its entire purpose is to make us imagine worst-case scenarios. It can cause us to catastrophize all the bad things that might happen should we take the scary, less-trodden route.

Upon realizing this, Poler decided to initiate a change.

"If we actually want to face a fear, and do it with the best attitude, we have to ask ourselves, 'What's the best that can happen?' instead of dwelling on the worst," Poler told me. When we think about the worst thing that could happen, our brain gets filled with negative thoughts and images that ignite our fears, worries, or anxieties. When we think about the best-case scenarios, the opposite happens. "We're reminded of the reasons why we thought that taking a risk was a good idea," Poler said. We might get a pay raise, we might have a really positive impact on our team, or we might feel a huge sense of pride (not to mention adrenaline) from having the courage to walk away from a demoralizing job.

Research published in the *Journal of Positive Psychology* supports this reframing. Duke University's Kathryn Adair Boulus, who led the research, found that when people thought about a positive event they hoped would happen in their future just six times in the space of a month, they reported feeling more resilient and less depressed compared to those who didn't.[1] Adair also found that when the "positive future event" group did experience disappointments, those feelings subsided more quickly.

In summary, the more confident we feel about uncertainty, the happier we feel in the present and the more prepared we are for the setbacks that life will inevitably throw our way in the future.

The next time you're feeling nervous about an event or activity you're tasked with doing, try it. Ask yourself, "What's the best thing that could happen?" Take a few minutes to think and write down your answer. Then spend some time really internalizing all the positive possibilities. Looking at your list will help you gather the courage to act—and to face your fear.

AMANTHA IMBER is the author of *Time Wise*, the founder of behavioral science consultancy Inventium, and the host of *How I Work*, a podcast about the habits and rituals of the world's most successful people.

## Notes

1. Kathryn C. Adair, Lindsay A. Kennedy, and J. Bryan Sexton, "Three Good Tools: Positively Reflecting Backwards and Forwards Is Associated with Robust Improvements in Well-Being Across Three Distinct Interventions," *Journal of Positive Psychology* 15, no. 5 (July 2020): 613–622.

Adapted from content posted on hbr.org, July 27, 2022.

# 5

# How to Stop Ruminating

By Alice Boyes

D o you ever find yourself endlessly mentally replaying situations in which you wish you'd performed differently? You wish you hadn't said something. You wish you'd volunteered for a project that's now winning accolades. You wish you'd spoken up. You wish you hadn't dropped the ball with a potential client.

Overthinking in this way is called rumination. While we worry about what might occur in the future, we ruminate about events that have already happened. A ruminative reaction to an event often triggers memories of similar situations from the past and an unproductive focus on the gap between the real and ideal self. Prompted by this one event, you begin to chastise yourself for not being more of something . . . organized, ambitious, smart, disciplined, or charismatic.

Rumination isn't just unpleasant. It's closely linked to poor problem-solving, anxiety, and depression. The good news is that there are effective solutions for breaking yourself out of this rut, and they're simpler than you might think.

## Identify your most common triggers

You can't quell rumination without noticing that you're doing it, but people aren't always able to spot it in themselves. A great way to get better at this is to think about what has triggered you in the past. Your list might look something like:

- Collaborating with people I don't yet trust

- Being around people who seem smarter or more ambitious

- Taking a step up in my career

- Making major money decisions

Notice if the dominant pattern of your rumination is blaming yourself or blaming others. Most heavy ruminators lean toward one or the other of these.

## Get psychological distance

Next, you need to put some psychological distance between you and the things you ruminate about. For instance, you might feel concerned about how you're perceived by people who have no impact on your success, get hung up about very small amounts of money, or see yourself as an underachiever despite the fact that objectively you're doing very well. One way to start to get this distance is by labeling what's running through your head as *thoughts and feelings*. So instead of saying "I'm inadequate," you might say, "I'm feeling like I'm inadequate." You can even be more lighthearted about it: "Oh, that's just my ruminating mind overheating again."

Recognizing the absurdity in some of your reactions can also help you take them less seriously. Look for any subtle entitlement or self-absorption hidden in your ruminations. Do you expect things to always go your way? Do you tend to believe people are scrutinizing you when, in reality, they're probably thinking about themselves? Do you spend time comparing yourself to business superstars or celebrities? Entitlement and personalizing can indicate that you tend to think the world revolves around you. If applicable, try to see the irony in being both narcissistic and insecure, rather than viewing it as an indictment on your character. You can even try imagining an over-the-top TV character version of yourself. Not every rumination topic is appropriate for this strategy but catch any that are.

# Distinguish between ruminating and problem-solving

Occasionally you might have a useful insight while ruminating, but mostly it's an avoidance to coping. Generally, the more people ruminate, the less effective they are at problem-solving. Either they don't think of solutions or don't pursue them quickly or effectively. For instance, one study showed that women who were heavy ruminators took over a month longer to seek medical care after finding a breast lump.[1] To shift from rumination to improvement mode, ask yourself, "What's the best choice right now, given the reality of the situation?" Start by taking one step, even if it's not the most perfect or comprehensive thing you could do. This strategy is particularly relevant for perfectionists. If you're ruminating about a mistake you've made, adopt a strategy that will lessen the likelihood of it happening again.

# Train your brain to become nonstick

As soon as you notice you're ruminating, try to distract yourself for a few minutes. Engage in an activity that's short and mentally absorbing but not extraordinarily difficult, like spending 10 minutes filling out an expense report. The activity you pick should be one that requires you to concentrate. In some situations, you might be able to just refocus your attention on what you're supposed to be doing. You might think: "How could something so simple help with my complex, emotional problem?" But this technique can be surprisingly effective.

Physical activity, such as jogging or walking, can also calm a mind that's prone to rumination. Meditation or yoga can be especially helpful for protecting yourself from sticky thoughts and learning not to overengage with them. These practices ask you to notice when your mind has wandered off to the past or future and bring it back to what's happening in the present (often your breathing or other sensations in your body or surroundings). This is exactly the skill you need for coping with moments of rumination.

## Check your thinking for errors

Sometimes rumination is triggered by cognitive errors. The catch-22 is that you're not likely to be very good at detecting distorted thinking when you're ruminating, since it clouds thinking. The solution is to develop a good understanding of your typical thinking errors, over time, in calm moments so that you're still able to recognize them when you're feeling heightened emotions. Here's a personal example: I'll often read a work-related email and zone in on one or two sentences that irritate or upset me and then misinterpret the overall tone of the message as demanding or dismissive. But, because I'm aware of this pattern, I've learned to not ruminate over my initial impressions. Instead, I read the email again after a day's cooldown and usually see that I had a biased impression of it.

Other common cognitive errors include setting too-high expectations for yourself, misinterpreting others' expectations of you, underestimating the extent to which other smart people struggle with what's troubling you, and making mountains out of molehills. If you're ruminating about someone else's behavior and attributing a cause to that behavior, at least entertain the idea that your explanation is wrong and try to accept that you might never know the truth. Recognizing that we often won't understand the reasons for someone else's behavior is a hugely important skill in reducing rumination.

Rumination is a widespread problem. Before you can break out of it, you need to become more aware of when you're doing it and have resistance strategies ready to go. This takes time and effort. But it's important—for your mental health and productivity—to try to nip it in the bud. So, before you go deep into your next "would have, should have, could have" spiral, give one or more of these ideas a go.

ALICE BOYES is a former clinical psychologist turned writer and the author of *The Healthy Mind Toolkit*, *The Anxiety Toolkit*, and *Stress-Free Productivity*.

## Notes

1. Sonja Lyubomirsky et al., "Ruminative Response Styles and Delay of Seeking Diagnosis for Breast Cancer Symptoms," *Journal of Social and Clinical Psychology* 25, no. 3 (2006): 276–304.

Adapted from "How to Stop Obsessing Over Your Mistakes" on hbr.org, February 25, 2019 (product #H04T7G).

# 6

# Breaking the Anxiety Loop

An interview with Judson Brewer by
Morra Aarons-Mele

t's never a bad time to think about habits. Why do we do what we do? What is and isn't healthy for us? What can we do to improve our lives?

Dr. Judson Brewer is an addiction psychiatrist, neuroscientist, and associate professor at the Brown University School of Public Health. He's also the author of the books *Unwinding Anxiety* and *The Craving Mind*. His research focuses on how and why your anxiety—and why worrying more specifically—might be a habit. In this interview, he explains the three-step process that forms this habit and how we can use curiosity to break out of the loop.

**Morra Aarons-Mele:** *You say that anxiety hides in our habits. How?*

**Judson Brewer:** Any habit is formed in a three-step process: First comes a trigger or cue, followed by a behavior, and then a reward. When our brain says "anxiety's unpleasant," that could be the cue. The associated behavior could be something physical, such as eating, or it could be mental, such as worrying.

In fact, worry is one of the biggest habit loops around anxiety. Research has shown that worrying tends to make people feel like they're in control, even if they're not, or like they're at least doing something, even if they don't have control over a situation. So, doing something, even if it's worrying, feels more productive than just waiting for whatever to happen; it's rewarding to our brain. That reward feeds back and tells us, "Hey, next time you're anxious, you should worry some more." That's how anxiety gets set up as a habit.

*Why does worrying feel productive to our brains?*

"Doing something" is the key piece here. There's also this fallacy of correlation that our brain assumes is causation. What it means is that we could be worrying and come up with a solution, but it doesn't mean that the worrying *caused* us to come up with a solution. There's plenty of research showing that when we worry, we actually narrow our focus and can't think creatively. We can't put ourselves in a growth mindset, and it hinders our problem-solving abilities. Essentially, the planning part of the brain is turned off.

*Let's use a workplace example. You get an email from your boss. You worry they're mad at you. How do we stop getting into these loops?*

When we see an email from our boss, our heart rate might actually go up without even looking at the subject line just because it's from our boss. Start mapping out the cue, trigger, and reward. Before you open the email, notice what you tend to do. Do you start to worry that you're in trouble? Do you think they're asking you to do more work? Are they going to ask you to cover for someone?

The second step is to simply ask ourselves, what am I getting from this behavior? What am I getting from worrying? Then, drop into your direct experience to see how rewarding it actually is—or isn't. What does it feel like to worry? For most people, it doesn't feel very good. So while you may think that worrying is going to help you get things done or solve a problem, if you look closely you realize that it probably isn't true. What we *do* know to be true is that worrying burns us out, and it makes us feel more anxious. So it feeds back and drives anxiety, and we start to become disenchanted with the worry itself.

*We're not trying to change the anxiety trigger at this point, right? We're not saying, "Don't read your email" or "Don't feel that way when you see your boss's name."*

Right, because often people get stuck in these loops of trying to control or avoid triggers. For example, if we don't read our boss's email, other consequences are probably going to happen that are going to add to our anxiety. You've got to deal with triggers.

But triggers don't drive habits. What does is how *rewarding* a behavior is (also known as reward-based learning). When something's rewarding, we're going to repeat it. If it's not rewarding, we're going to stop doing it, and that has nothing to do with the trigger.

*So what should you do?*

Get curious. When you get that email, instead of getting lost and catastrophizing, ask yourself, what am I getting from this behavior? What does anxiety feel like as compared to worrying?

Curiosity feels better. And in that moment, the curiosity not only feels better, it's also more rewarding. It helps us step out of that old worry habit loop. You can dwell on questions like, "What does this anxiety feel like in my body right now, as compared to worrying about the future?" Notice what thoughts are coming up. Are you feeling contracted or closed down? Where are you feeling it? Is it on the left side? In the front? The back? This sparks your natural ability to be curious, helps you be present and feel centered, and avoids feeding the anxiety habit loop. Then take a deep breath, calm down a little bit, and open up that email. You'll find that instead of thinking, "My boss is emailing me, what's wrong?" you'll think, "I wonder what they'd like to communicate to me?" Essentially, it helps you be in a very different mindset instead of catastrophizing.

JUDSON BREWER is a psychiatrist and neuroscientist, and the author of *Unwinding Anxiety: New Science Shows How to Break the Cycles of Worry and Fear to Heal Your Mind.* MORRA AARONS-MELE is the founder of the award-winning social impact agency Women Online and author of *Hiding in the Bathroom* and *The Anxious Achiever.* She has written for the *New York Times;* the *Wall Street Journal; O, the Oprah Magazine;* and other publications.

Adapted from "Anxiety Is a Habit," *The Anxious Achiever* (podcast) December 6, 2021.

# 7

# Use Gratitude to Counter Stress and Uncertainty

By Christopher Littlefield

iving in a constant state of uncertainty—a pandemic, a looming recession, or layoffs—can feel like running a race with no finish line or completing a puzzle without a reference picture. Everything seems unclear, and the worst seems possible.

Of course, this not a fun state of mind to be in. So what can we possibly do to help minimize the impacts of uncertainty on our well-being? While it may not address the root cause, research shows that gratitude can help balance us out.[1]

# Why is gratitude important?

"Gratitude is an emotion that grounds us and is a great way to balance out the negative mindset that uncertainty engenders," said Dr. Guy Winch, author of the book *Emotional First Aid*. When we express gratitude, our brain releases dopamine and serotonin—two hormones that make us feel lighter and happier inside.

We experience gratitude when we shift our focus from what we don't have to what we do, and when we take time to appreciate and be thankful for those who have contributed to the abundance in our lives. Nearly a decade of research by Dr. Robert Emmons—the world's leading scientific expert on gratitude—and others has found that people who have regular gratitude practices are healthier, are happier, and have better relationships. Further research suggests that gratitude is also key in helping individuals and teams persevere in challenging tasks.

Think of your mind like your digestive system— what you put in it impacts how you feel. When you flood your mind with a constant flow of worry, envy, resentment, and self-criticism (compounded by a barrage of news and other media) it negatively impacts your mental well-being. A gratitude practice is like a workout and a healthy eating plan for your mind.

In his article "Why Gratitude Is Good," Emmons writes, "You can't feel envious and grateful at the same time. They're incompatible feelings, because if you're grateful, you can't resent someone for owning things you don't." He goes on to share his research, which found that people with high levels of gratitude have low levels of resentment and envy. (For more on these feelings, see the sidebar "The Relationship Between Envy and Anxiety.") When we take time to focus on what we are grateful for, we choose positive emotions over negative; thus, we take steps to nurture our mental health and well-being.

How do we trigger gratitude in ourselves? It's simple. We take time to shift our focus.

## How to trigger gratitude in ourselves

Have you ever noticed that when you are looking to buy a new phone, jacket, or some other object all of a sudden everyone around you has it? That's because, consciously or unconsciously, whatever we are focused on is what we see. If we want to trigger gratitude in ourselves, we need to intentionally shift our focus to that which we are grateful for. The simplest way to do this is through questions, prompts, and a few daily rituals.

## THE RELATIONSHIP BETWEEN ENVY AND ANXIETY

*By Nihar Chhaya*

Envy and anxiety are a bit of a chicken-and-egg situation. If I'm in an anxious state and feeling down on myself, I'm probably more susceptible to the cues and signals of other people, which can make me wonder, "Am I keeping up with other folks?"

On the other hand, I remember some bouts with anxiety when I wasn't envying what other people had, but instead had a feeling of, "Am I going to lose the freedom and autonomy that I've worked so hard to have?" which was to start my own company. For any reason, whether fear of not having enough clients or that something might happen to me (like a health issue or an injury), all of a sudden I'm imagining that everybody else has it perfect. Those who work in companies are happy, and those who have their own

*(Continued)*

businesses are happy. I'm the one that's not going to excel. It's at that point that I'm susceptible to envy.

If you start envying people, then you're susceptible to feeling more anxious. Where the anxiety comes in is when there are things that you want or when you covet what other people have with some level of urgency or scarcity associated with it. So if there's an urgency—in other words "I need to make a certain amount of money by the next six months to break even"—you're going to start feeling more anxious about what you see other people doing.

Or consider scarcity. In my world of coaching there are a million coaches out there, and every year more and more people hang up a shingle and say, "I want to start my own practice." In this case, you start thinking, "How do I stand out? How do I actually make sure I'm differentiating in this saturated market?" That's where the scarcity element can wreak havoc in your mind, and the envy and anxiety play off of each other into a circular loop.

**Nihar Chhaya** is an executive coach to senior leaders at global companies, including American Airlines, Coca-Cola, DraftKings, and Wieden+Kennedy. A former *Fortune* 500 corporate head of talent development, he is the president of PartnerExec, helping leaders master influence for superior business and strategic outcomes.

Adapted from "Understanding Envy Part 1: How Envy Impacts Anxiety and Leadership," *The Anxious Achiever* (podcast), December 14, 2020.

## *Pause and reflect*

When you find yourself stuck in a constant state of worry or hyper-focused on what is not working around you, pause for a second and ask yourself one or two of the following questions:

- What opportunities do I currently have that I am grateful for?

- What have I gotten to learn recently that has helped me grow?

- What physical abilities do I have but take for granted?

- What did I see today or over the last month that was beautiful?

- Who at work am I happy to see each day and why?

- Who is a person that I don't speak to often, but, if I lost them tomorrow, it would be devastating? (Take this as a cue to reach out today!)

- What am I better at today than I was a year ago?

- What material object do I use every day that I am thankful for having?

- What has someone done for me recently that I am grateful for?

- What are the three things I am grateful for right now?

By taking time to write down our answers, we consciously redirect our attention to that which we are grateful for. It's also a great way to look back and realize what we may have thought of as insignificant was actually that which brought us joy.

### *Write a gratitude journal*

One common practice is to keep a daily gratitude journal. Jae Ellard, the founder of the mindful-based consulting company Simple Intentions, recommends bookending your day with thoughts of gratitude. She recommends carving out a few minutes at the beginning and end of the day for reflection. Maybe it is gratitude for the fresh pomegranate you had with your yogurt or for the health of your family. Winch suggests starting the practice of "writing one paragraph every day about one thing for which we're truly grateful and why that thing is meaningful to us." He says, "This introduces positive thoughts and feelings into an emotional climate that is tipped too much toward the negative." We can also focus our gratitude exercise on the meaningful things in our lives of which we are certain—our friendships, passions, or family—thereby reminding ourselves that while uncertainty exists in some aspects of our lives, certainty still prevails in many others.

### *Build it in like a routine*

I recently came across someone who has taken on the practice of sharing one picture a day on LinkedIn of something he is grateful for and tells his audience the reason behind it. His daily practice not only helps him focus on the positive but inspires others to do the same.

Another way to create a ritual around gratitude is to start or end each virtual meeting or co-study session with a grateful minute. Pick any one or two questions outlined earlier and invite a few team members or friends to share their answers.

If we want to be able to keep running in this race with no clear finish line, we need to learn to take better care of the runner. Although there is no one solution, learning to trigger gratitude may help us cope along the way.

CHRISTOPHER LITTLEFIELD is an international and TEDx speaker specializing in employee appreciation and the founder of Beyond Thank You. He has trained thousands of leaders across six continents to create cultures where people feel valued every day. He is the author of *75+ Team Building Activities for Remote Teams: Simple Ways to Build Trust, Strengthen Communication, and Laugh Together from Afar.*

## Notes

1. Summer Allen, "The Science of Gratitude," Greater Good Science Center at UC Berkeley, May 2018, https://ggsc .berkeley.edu/images/uploads/GGSC-JTF_White_Paper -Gratitude-FINAL.pdf.

Adapted from content posted on hbr.org, October 20, 2020.

# 8

# How to Manage a Panic Attack at Work

An interview with Sridevi Kalidindi by
Vasundhara Sawhney

lost my father unexpectedly in May 2022, on a quiet Sunday morning. I cried my heart out, alone, in my bathroom. Being the older of two siblings, I took it upon myself to put my brave face on and be there for my mother and my sister. At some point during the day, and while carrying out the rituals, I forgot how to feel pain. Those who saw me said I looked robotic. After a week of staying home with my mother and trying to get her back up on her feet, I picked up my laptop and walked to work. I pretended like nothing happened. I walked around the office, telling everyone, "It's business as usual," "I'm my dad's daughter and he would've wanted me to get back to work," and "Death isn't the end."

In the week that followed, work became my therapy. I spent endless hours at my desk, submerged in work, the only thing keeping me sane at the time. I was barely sleeping. The minute I closed my eyes I'd see my father. And I didn't want to. I tanked up on caffeine in the mornings and through the workday to appear hyperalert. No one could tell I was grieving.

A week after my father's death, I had to travel abroad for a work trip. Everyone, including my manager, felt I wasn't ready to be alone. "Of course, I'm absolutely OK," I told them. My grieving was less intense than I had thought it would be, and I didn't want anyone to think less of me and my confidence. I boarded the flight.

I was by myself for the first time since my father passed away. I was sleeping with the lights turned on. I found peace in crowded cafés because the chatter drowned out my thoughts. I was constantly thinking about my mother. What if she needed me? Was my sister OK? Was it OK to be so far away from them right now?

Three days into my trip, just as I was finishing my evening run in Harvard Square, my body went into a panic. There was no pain. Just cold sweats, shortness of breath, and an inexplicable sensation. If I didn't know better, I'd call it a heart attack. I drank all the water I had on me, booked an Uber, and went back to my hotel. Was I dying? I was in a country I didn't call home. My friends and family were a 20-hour flight away. What was I supposed to do?

After 20 minutes of deep breathing, panting and huffing, pacing up and down the lobby, I decided to call my manager. "I'm really embarrassed to tell you this, but something is wrong. I can't breathe," I said in a low, trembling voice. "Talk to me. What are you feeling?" she said. It was the most vulnerable I'd ever been to anyone at work. But it was also the calmest I'd ever felt.

A few hours later, I got on my flight back home. Knowing I was on my way home brought back some semblance of normalcy to my otherwise shallow breathing.

Panic attacks, like the one I had, don't come with a warning. They can be especially traumatizing if you're alone, or at work. But they can happen to anyone, and they can happen at any time.

I reached out to Dr. Sridevi Kalidindi, a national clinical leader, award-winning consultant psychiatrist of many years, and an executive coach based in the United Kingdom, to understand what we should know about panic attacks and what we can do when going through one.

**Vasundhara Sawhney:** *What causes a panic attack?*

**Sridevi Kalidindi:** Panic attacks are caused by your sympathetic nervous system being stimulated. We process fearful and threatening stimuli in our amygdala. When emotions of fear and threat arise, your brain springs into action, making you believe you're in mortal danger. A cascade of chemicals, including adrenaline and cortisol, are released into your bloodstream. This takes you into "fight, flight, freeze, or appease" mode. You might breathe more quickly to take in more oxygen, your heart beats faster, and you're highly alert to your surroundings.

## *What does it feel like and what are the symptoms?*

A panic attack can feel like impending doom, quite literally as though you are going to die. The physical symptoms and cognitive symptoms include rapid and concurrent onset of a number of characteristic symptoms, which may include, but are not limited to, palpitations or increased heart rate, sweating, trembling, sensations of shortness of breath, feelings of choking, chest pain, nausea or abdominal distress, feelings of dizziness or light headedness, chills or hot flushes, tingling or lack of sensation in extremities (i.e., paresthesias), depersonalization or derealization, fear of losing control, and fear of imminent death.[1]

Panic attacks can appear out of the blue, and some may be triggered by particular situations. This is then followed by persistent worry that the panic attack may reoccur, leading to avoidance of the situation and other safety-seeking behaviors, which are unnecessary actions employed to stop a feared catastrophe.

*Are they common after big life events, especially when you still need to process?*

When emotions like grief are not processed and instead repressed, it may lead to the emotions being internalized and showing up in other ways. By carrying on as normal with work and life and not taking the time to allow your mind, body, and spirit to process the huge and sudden loss you experienced from the passing of your father, you were avoiding and repressing your feelings.

In your case, travelling for work, too, was a part of this avoidance. There is a reason that many cultures have a time of mourning after the death of a loved one. It is to allow time to process, together with other loved ones, your loss and to adjust to it. Bereavements, too, trigger low mood and anxiety as part of the stages of grief.

*What can we do in the moment, say, if we're at work?*

It is possible to start to feel a panic attack coming on. The kinds of symptoms can be different for each person, but they usually include a combination of the symptoms I described. But it's also important to ensure that those symptoms aren't due to another medical condition (an adrenaline-producing tumor) or the direct effects of a substance or medication on the central nervous system (e.g., coffee, cocaine), including withdrawal effects (e.g., alcohol, benzodiazepines). An underlying depression may also lead to anxiety symptoms and panic attacks.

If you're feeling any of these symptoms, first, take a deep breath. Know that the symptoms may be unpleasant, but they will pass. Now tell yourself that the sensation being felt is likely normal bodily sensations, such as a muscle twinge, and not a serious health condition, so as not to cause an increased stimulation of the fight-or-flight system. That could cause further release of chemicals, thereby increasing the physical symptoms.

Next, try self-soothing techniques, which activate the parasympathetic nervous system (the network of nerves in your body that help you relax, especially after stressful episodes). Here are two ways to do that.

- Practice "square breathing." This involves imagining your breathing as a square—breathe in for four seconds, hold your breath for four, then out for four and hold for four again. You can continue to do this until you're feeling calmer. As you intentionally slow down and control your breathing, your heart rate will come down, the tingling sensations that come with over-breathing settle, and gradually, the panic attack subsides.

- Be present in the moment. In moments like these, mindfulness can be helpful too. When you're feeling panicky, pay attention to your current experience. What's happening to you? What are the sensations in your body? What are you feeling? Notice your thoughts: Imagine yourself on the bank of a river, with your thoughts flowing past in the river. Know you do not need to attach yourself to any one of those thoughts. Let them pass. Just focus on the present moment's experience, using all of your senses and not your thoughts.

*What should we absolutely not do?*

First, try not to leave the situation you are in where you are experiencing the panic attack. The reason for this is that when you stay in the situation, the anxiety will plateau and then subside naturally. This may take a long time initially. Once you've experienced it, it should become quicker, until hopefully, it may completely subside.

Next, try not to employ other safety-seeking behaviors—unnecessary actions which we instinctively employ to stop a feared catastrophe—to try and assign meaning to the particular circumstances present at the time. For example, you may leave a room you feel has triggered a panic attack as it brought back certain memories.

The issue with this is that if one leaves the stressful stimulus before the anxiety settles down again, which it naturally will, then you start to believe the panic attack was averted due to the safety behavior. You may start to avoid that particular setting and repeat the safety behavior—leaving the room every time bodily sensations are felt and misinterpreted. It can lead to limitation of aspects of one's life. For some it can become very debilitating in terms of everyday functioning, even leading to people becoming housebound in severe cases.

*What if someone else is having a panic attack. How can we help them? Are there things we should do or phrases we shouldn't use?*

The first thing is to speak with them to try and understand what is happening if possible. If they and you are unsure as to what is happening and there are a lot of physical symptoms, ensure there is no underlying physical health issue related to the symptoms. For example, in a heart attack, the pain is classically described as central, causing chest pain ("like an elephant sitting on your chest"), radiating down the left arm and the jaw and maybe to the back too.

If it is someone who is known to have panic attacks and they are aware this is what is occurring, first help them get their breathing under control. Walk them through square breathing or just a simple inhale-exhale, asking them to focus on just their breath.

Next, help them become more present by saying something like, "Could you count backward in threes for me?" or "Would you describe for me what you're seeing around the room?"

Lastly, be kind, nonjudgmental, and helpful. This will go a long way toward helping people learn how to manage panic attacks on their own and to know that it is okay to go through one.

*I also feel that the fear of having another panic attack is keeping me from doing certain things, like traveling alone. Is there a way to combat this?*

The best treatment for the fear of having another panic attack is cognitive behavioral therapy and exposure work, and medication may also be needed. By practicing breath meditation and mindfulness you will strengthen your ability to use these techniques should another panic attack begin.

Exposure work involves deliberate confrontation of the feared situation in reality and/or your imagination. This can be self-directed or accompanied—by a therapist, for example. There are different methods that may be used such as gradual exposure to the feared situation, or one can be flooded in a one-off exposure of the whole situation/stimulus.

In moderate to severe cases of panic disorder, medication, such as SSRIs, can also support treatment of the condition. Therapeutic work should also take place in conjunction with the medication for it to be effective and sustainable.

SRIDEVI KALIDINDI is a national clinical leader, award-winning consultant psychiatrist, and an executive coach based in the United Kingdom. VASUNDHARA SAWHNEY is a senior editor at *Harvard Business Review*.

## Notes

1. "Panic Attacks and Panic Disorder," Mayo Clinic, May 4, 2018, https://www.mayoclinic.org/diseases-conditions/panic-attacks/symptoms-causes/syc-20376021.

Adapted from content posted on hbr.org, January 23, 2023.

# 9

# Anxious About What's Next? Here's How to Cope

By Rasmus Hougaard and Jacqueline Carter

Transitions—graduations, first days at a new job, strategic planning for the next fiscal year—often bring a mix of anticipation and excitement. You don't exactly know what lies ahead, but you're eager to get there nonetheless.

These liminal periods—at the boundary of a new state or experience—are complex spaces to occupy. They can make us feel untethered and disoriented. But at the same time, they have great potential. The gift of transition is the opportunity for self-reflection, growth, and change. If we approach work and life transitions with the right mindset, they can be hugely rewarding.

So how do you gain greater clarity of mind when maneuvering new territory?

## Don't think, just be

The human mind believes falsely that it can think its way through a period of uncertainty. We are convinced that by understanding the source of uncertainty, we can somehow fix it. But it doesn't work that way. On the contrary, by overanalyzing, we make matters worse, like throwing water on a grease fire in hopes of extinguishing the flames.

In liminal periods, our brain defaults to survival mode. The heightened levels of uncertainty and angst trigger our amygdala which in turn reacts in one of two ways: fighting or fleeing. We either try to escape the feelings of anxiety and fear, or we try to wrestle with the thoughts through knowledge-gathering and problem-solving.

Many people operating in survival mode walk around with a "let's think our way through this crisis" mentality. But this hyper-analytic mindset can backfire and lead to obsessive rumination and worry.[1] Trying to think our way out of the crisis directs our attention, over and over, to thoughts and feelings that fuel the initial anxiety. We get caught in a negative, downward spiral that leaves us less focused for the new period ahead.

Breaking this cycle starts by letting go of the overthinking and instead getting comfortable with just *being* and experiencing our emotions as they come. We will not find all the answers to our questions about what is to come, but we will find greater self-discovery and an ability to direct our mind toward more calm, resilience, and focus.

## Turn outward, not inward

The amygdala hijack we experience during a transition throws us another curveball: It makes us self-centered.

Research shows that anxious states of mind can cause individuals to display greater egocentric thinking and behaviors.[2] When a person feels the mounting pressure of uncertainty, the ensuing anxiety biases their view of the world so that they see only themselves and their own distress. Equally detrimental, research shows that anxiety degrades our ability for perspective-taking. In other words, we fail to see things from another's point of view.

Sadly, to survive a crisis or transition, our minds reject or ignore the very things that would allow us to feel grounded and connected. Instead of reaching out for community and connection, we draw inward and focus on our own situations versus others'. Breaking this pattern can be as simple as making a compassionate gesture or a phone call to someone who is struggling. A 2016 study found that when we treat others with a gift, we become happier and more resilient than if we gave ourselves the same gift. In this way, caring for others is a wise form of self-interest—especially in a crisis.[3]

It is ironic that what is likely to get us through these difficult times are the complete opposites of what our default psychology is pushing us to do. We need to understand ourselves rather than overthink the situation. And we need to consider the needs of others above our own. Human beings are just that: human *beings*, not human doings. And our common humanity means we share in this struggle together.

The good news is that we can train ourselves to rewire our default psychology and move through the threshold with greater self-awareness, focus, and resilience.

# Rewire the mind through self-discovery

We can, in a sense, reprogram our default reactions. In fact, our own research has shown that we can do this in only 10 minutes.[4] The best place to begin is with an understanding of how your own mind works. For example, do you know the answers to these questions?

- What parts of the day bring the highest levels of focus, energy, and productivity for you?

- When does your mind wander away into worry and stress? What are the triggers for you?

- How does sleep affect your mood and your response to challenging moments?

- Do you feel comforted and more resilient with alone time or time with others?

- Do you know whether you're making the right decisions based on your personality style?

With greater awareness, you can then take action. For example, knowing your unique pattern of focus during the day can help you to plan your day accordingly. You can proactively schedule important activities and meetings at the times when your focus is strongest and save more passive tasks for the hours when your focus is weaker. Similarly, once you uncover what deepens or depletes your levels of resilience, the more you can adopt resilience-building practices, like getting good quality sleep and connecting with others around you.

Technology can come in handy in the pursuit of greater self-awareness. At Potential Project, we developed an app called "mindgrow," which can help you track the ups and downs of your focus and resilience during a typical work week. The personalized

Mind Discovery Report includes specific tips for breaking automatic patterns and rewiring your mind for life during this period of uncertainty and change. Here are a few to get you started:

Create a ritual to set intention and focus attention. We're all so busy, we naturally look for opportunities to complete tasks on autopilot. The brain opts for this type of auto-mode because it helps to reserve conscious cognitive resources. But left unchecked, autopilot can become the dominant mode, which is not good. A ritual helps to set an intention at the beginning or end of a work session/task or to reorient your attention to a focal task.

Be fully present with those around you. Whether you're on a Zoom call or in a conversation, keep your attention on the topic and the person you're with. Ask yourself: What is the other person feeling? What are they needing? And what are you feeling? If you find it hard to keep your focus, ask a question to reengage your attention.

Pay more attention to daily "sense" experiences around you. Every now and then, take a few minutes to notice the sounds around you, the taste of your food, or the wind on your face when you're outside. Pausing occasionally to observe what your five senses are telling you can offer both a refuge from a busy mind and a way to enhance your awareness.

———————

There are no clear answers for what our work lives will look like. We can only guess, hope, worry and wonder. But conquering our anxiety and braving the uncertain world that lies ahead means being intentional about what we think and how we react. We can find multiple paths of self-discovery within our own minds, if only we stop and take a look.

RASMUS HOUGAARD is the founder and CEO of Potential Project, a global leadership, organizational development, and research firm serving Microsoft, Accenture, Cisco, and hundreds of other organizations. JACQUELINE CARTER is a partner and the North American Director of Potential Project. They are coauthors of *Compassionate Leadership: How to Do Hard Things in a Human Way* and *The Mind of the Leader: How to Lead Yourself, Your People, and Your Organization for Extraordinary Results* (both Harvard Business Review Press, 2022 and 2018, respectively).

# Notes

1. Louisa C. Michl et al., "Rumination as a Mechanism Linking Stressful Life Events to Symptoms of Depression and Anxiety: Longitudinal Evidence in Early Adolescents and Adults," *Journal of Abnormal Psychology* 122, no. 2 (2013): 339–352.
2. Andrew R. Todd et al., "Anxious and Egocentric: How Specific Emotions Influence Perspective Taking," *Journal of Experimental Psychology* 144, no. 2 (2015): 374–391.
3. S. Katherine Nelson et al., "Do Unto Others or Treat Yourself? The Effects of Prosocial and Self-Focused Behavior on Psychological Flourishing," *Emotion* 16, no. 6 (2016): 850–861.
4. Rasmus Hougaard, "The Power of 10 Minutes: How Mindfulness Can Address the Looming Mental Health Crisis

in Businesses," *Forbes*, June 9, 2020, https://www.forbes
.com/sites/rasmushougaard/2020/06/09/the-power-of
-10-minutes-how-mindfulness-can-address-the-looming
-mental-health-crisis-in-businesses/.

Adapted from content posted on hbr.org, August 5, 2020
(product #H05RKW).

# 10

# What Does Self-Compassion Really Mean?

By Stephanie Harrison

One Friday morning, early in my career, an email popped into my inbox. It was a client, inquiring about a weekly report. With a dawning sense of horror, I realized that I had completely forgotten to make and send it.

I quickly pulled the report together and sent it over, expressing how sorry I was for my mistake. My client couldn't have been nicer about it. Despite their kindness, my internal voice couldn't stop berating me: "How could you have made this mistake? What's wrong with you? I knew you weren't cut out for this job."

Think back to the last time you made a mistake or had a setback at work. How did you respond? If, like me, you were extremely self-critical, ashamed, and stressed, or perceived yourself as a less worthy professional (or person), I want you to know that you're not alone.

## Why are we so hard on ourselves?

Many of us have been raised to accept that, to be successful, we have to be perfect. This perfectionism is often grounded in beliefs like, "I should never struggle to perform," "I always have to get it right," or "I have to be the best at everything." To be clear, those standards are impossible to meet—and often, detrimental to our success and well-being.

Studies show that perfectionism has significantly increased over the last two decades, to a dangerous effect.[1] Young people hold unrealistic standards for themselves, as well as those around them. This perfectionism, in part, is driven by the societies we live in and the medias we regularly consume, many of which emphasize social comparison. Internalizing such idealism negatively affects everyone, but especially younger generations who are likely to be more depressed, more burned out, and less productive than the generations before them.[2] The same research also highlights that perfectionism is a leading cause of increased anxiety and depression among young people in the United States, the U.K., and Canada.

The truth is that mistakes, setbacks, and challenges are an inevitable part of our working lives. More importantly, they are necessary. There's no way to grow, contribute, or make a difference without stumbling a little. Instead of meeting your mistakes with self-criticism, there's a far better option: self-compassion.

## What is self-compassion, and how does it work?

Self-compassion is a way of relating to yourself that is derived from Buddhist psychology. It was pioneered in academic research by professor Kristin Neff, who breaks self-compassion into three key components:[3]

- *Self-kindness:* treating yourself with care and understanding

- *Mindfulness:* accurately perceiving your thoughts, feelings, and experiences, without overidentifying with them

- *A sense of common humanity:* recognizing that challenges are a part of the human experience

Self-compassion has many benefits. It reduces feelings of anxiety and depression and improves your mental health. It makes you more resilient and adaptable. It helps you become more efficient and creative. Avoiding being harsh on yourself for every small misstep helps you overcome your fear of failure, admit mistakes, view them as a learning opportunity, and find new and creative solutions to move forward. In fact, a recent study also found that on days when employees were more self-compassionate, they made more progress on their goals and felt a greater sense of meaning at work.[4]

That said, learning how to be kind to yourself takes time, effort, and practice. Here is a four-step strategy that I've developed to help me cut myself some slack and become more self-compassionate: CARE.

## C: Catch yourself being critical

Often, our internal thoughts can feel like persistent background noise and be hard to turn off. One way to turn them down is to listen to this noise with patience and care.

The next time you make a mistake, start observing the critical things you say to yourself. For example:

- After noticing a typo in an email, you may say: "That was so irresponsible of me."

- After submitting your work, you may say: "That work wasn't good enough."

- After speaking in a meeting, you may say: "That comment I made was so unnecessary."

Bringing attention to these thoughts, in the moment that they come up, will help you identify them for what they are: just a critical or negative thought. When you notice yourself spiraling, stop and gently remind yourself: "That's a very critical thought."

While this action may seem small, it's a significant first step. Only when we acknowledge the things that bother us can we begin to change them. So, think of this step as a critical intervention to learning how to treat yourself with more compassion.

## A: Acknowledge your experiences

When critical thoughts arise, they are typically born from bigger, underlying feelings. Delving deeper into what's causing you to feel bad about yourself may be uncomfortable, so take your time.

There are several different challenges that we face at work. There are the big ones—losing a customer, not getting a promotion you had hoped for, or being laid off. Then, there are the smaller ones—a conflict with a coworker, a missed deadline, or forgetting to do something. In each of these moments, it's completely normal to feel emotions like frustration, grief, anger, or sadness. While you might be tempted to suppress your emotions, a better strategy is to engage with them mindfully.

This practice is called *emotional labeling* and refers to identifying your emotions without judgment or reprimand. Instead of just acknowledging that you're being unkind to yourself, like you did in the previous step, take a step further here to identify the emotions you're feeling. The goal is to validate your experience and affirm your feelings, instead of running away from them.

For instance, if you missed a deadline, pay attention to your feelings. Are you angry? Sad? Upset? Frustrated? As you think more about this, say out loud to yourself: "I feel angry," or "I feel disappointed."

Stating what you feel out loud quiets the amygdala and other limbic areas of the brain that are responsible for emotional processing. When you start paying attention to your emotions, it helps you see your feelings while making room for kindness.

## R: Request your own compassion

Now, ask yourself: "What would my most supportive friend say to me at this moment?"

It's most likely that your friend will reassure you that you're strong, intelligent, and capable; that you will bounce back from this challenge; and that you are loved, no matter what happens at work.

Visualize this situation, and try saying these words to yourself, with the same care and understanding.

If it feels silly or awkward believing this, gain confidence from the fact that if your friend were to go through what you just experienced, you'd also use similar words for them.

Another way to request kindness from yourself is to create a simple mantra that grounds you in reality and releases you from the expectation of having to be perfect. Here are a few examples:

- "I made a mistake today. But I'm not alone. Everyone stumbles and blunders."

- "Making a mistake makes me human. I'm allowed to err."

- "I'm letting go of the unkind expectation that I'm the only person in the world who can't make mistakes."

As you say these words to yourself, take deep breaths, put your hand on your heart, or close your eyes. Let yourself really feel this act of kindness, just like you would if it was coming from a loved one.

# E: Explore the best next step

The CARE strategy is not only good for your well-being. It can also help you be creative and find new solutions to the problem you're facing. That's because compassion activates your parasympathetic nervous system, which reduces your stress and facilitates a more adaptive response to challenges. No matter your challenge, there *is* a way to move forward, and you'll be far more likely to find it if you're kind to yourself first.

Once you've offered yourself compassion, pause and ask: "What's one step I can take to improve this situation?"

For instance, if you forget to complete an important weekly task, think of ways to avoid that mistake in the future. You could, for instance, add a reminder or block an hour each week to work on the task. You can even send a reminder to all your team members if it's a shared responsibility to ensure that the task is part of everyone's agenda. Instead of taking on blame for your mistakes, use the incident as a lesson to find systemic and lasting solutions—something that everyone can benefit from.

If you're used to criticizing yourself, self-compassion might feel foreign at first. Think of it as a muscle: The more you practice, the stronger it will become. Whenever you have a hard time extending yourself some grace, remember this: You deserve your own kindness.

STEPHANIE HARRISON is an expert in well-being and the founder of The New Happy, a platform helping millions of people to experience greater happiness. She's a designer, speaker, and writer. Her book *New Happy* will be published in 2024.

## Notes

1. Thomas Curran and Andrew P. Hill, "Perfectionism Is Increasing over Time: A Meta-Analysis of Birth Cohort Differences from 1989 to 2016," *Psychology Bulletin* 145, no. 4 (2019): 410–429.
2. Murray W. Enns and Brian J. Cox, "Perfectionism, Stressful Life Events, and the 1-Year Outcome of Depression,"

*Cognitive Therapy and Research* 29 (2005): 541–553; Andrew P. Hill and Thomas Curran, "Multidimensional Perfectionism and Burnout: A Meta-Analysis," *Personality and Social Psychology Review* 20, no. 3 (2016): 269–288.

3. Kristin Neff, "Self-Compassion: An Alternative Conceptualization of a Healthy Attitude Toward Oneself," *Self and Identity* 2, no. 2 (2003): 85–101.

4. Kristin D. Neff, "The Role of Self-Compassion in Development: A Healthier Way to Relate to Oneself," *Human Development* 52, no. 4 (2009): 211–214; Mark R. Leary et al., "Self-Compassion and Reactions to Unpleasant Self-Relevant Events: The Implications of Treating Oneself Kindly," *Journal of Personality and Social Psychology* 92, no. 5 (2007): 887–904; Kristin D. Neff, Ya-Ping Hsieh, and Kullaya Dejitterat, "Self-Compassion, Achievement Goals, and Coping with Academic Failure," *Self and Identity* 4, no. 3 (2005): 263–287; Juliana G. Breines and Serena Chen, "Self-Compassion Increases Self-Improvement Motivation," *Personality and Social Psychology Bulletin* 38, no. 9 (2012): 1133–1143; Remy E. Jennings, Klodiana Lanaj, and You Jin (YJ) Kim, "Self-Compassion at Work: A Self-Regulation Perspective on Its Beneficial Effects for Work Performance and Well-being," *Personnel Psychology* 76, no. 1 (2022): 279-309.

Adapted from content posted on hbr.org, December 12, 2022.

# Index

# How to be human at work.

HBR's Emotional Intelligence Series features smart, essential reading on the human side of professional life from the pages of *Harvard Business Review*. Each book in the series offers uplifting stories, practical advice, and research from leading experts on how to tend to our emotional well-being at work.

## Harvard Business Review Emotional Intelligence Series

**Available in paperback or ebook format. The specially priced six-volume set includes:**

- Mindfulness
- Resilience
- Influence and Persuasion

- Authentic Leadership
- Happiness
- Empathy